SECRETS

of owning a
successful hair company

DALANDRA YOUNG

Permission should be addressed in writing to Dalandra Young at
Dalandrayoung@gmail.com

Editor: Corinne Casazza
corinnecasazza@gmail.com

Cover & Book Design: Anne Karklins
anne@hasmarkpublishing.com

ISBN 13: 978-1-989161-89-0
ISBN 10: 1989161898

Hasmark
PUBLISHING

To you, the Reader
It is my honor and privilege to serve.

ACKNOWLEDGEMENTS

To my family,

Thank you for always standing behind me while I
find my perfect voice in this life.

Dalandra

TABLE OF CONTENTS

Chapter ONE	General Business Knowledge and Advice	11
Chapter TWO	Let's Talk about Hair	17
Chapter THREE	Hair Care	31
Chapter FOUR	Let's Get to Business	37
Chapter FIVE	Let's Make Some Money	43
Chapter SIX	Marketing	49
Chapter SEVEN	Your Image	57
Chapter EIGHT	In Closing	63

INTRODUCTION

I would personally like to congratulate you on starting your own hair company! My name is Dalandra Young, and I am one of the owners of Boss Xtend and Dropship Lengths. In this book I will share with you some information I learned from owning a hair company. There are no limits as to what you can do if you put your mind and the correct actions to it. You will get where you want to be in no time!

These views are my own and are based on the experiences I had while running my businesses. When we started, my daughter and I had no clue what we were doing, and we lost a lot of money in the process. I wanted to help teach others through my mistakes how to become a successful hair company without losing so much in the process.

I would like for you to take in as much information from me as possible, add it to your own creativity, and then apply the necessary actions to live the lifestyle of your dreams. I would like for you to also one day help someone change their life with your experience. Let's keep this going!

CHAPTER ONE

WHAT STOPS PEOPLE FROM STARTING THEIR OWN HAIR BUSINESS?

Through speaking to thousands of people since we started our hair company journey, I have come to the understanding there are a lot of issues that stop a person from starting their own business or reaching their true potential. I have listed some of the subjects I have come across while talking with others.

NOT KNOWING WHERE TO START

Most people who start a business do not know where to begin. Relax, this is normal. Sometimes we know where we want to be in life, but just don't know how to get there. When it comes to starting a hair business, I did a lot of research and watched many documentaries of people starting their hair companies. I wanted to know what they went through in the beginning. I wanted to know if all my fears were normal. I wanted to know if I was on track with what I was going through versus what they were going through at the time.

I followed a lot of hair company pages on social media while taking in as much information as I could. Normally I would go down to the very first post of a company just to see what content was displayed. I wanted to know what attracted others to their pages. I paid attention to what attracted me to their page. I studied the way they were advertising and what was working for them.

Once I was comfortable with what it seemed like I should be doing by comparing strategies from countless companies, I then looked up vendors and started in where I stood by asking as many questions as came to my mind. You have to remember that no question is a dumb question and this is absolutely how you learn. If you want to be knowledgeable about a business you have to make sure you ask questions, because believe me your customers will ask you and you have to be ready.

I DON'T KNOW ANYTHING ABOUT HAIR EXTENSIONS

I'm here to tell you firsthand that when we started this company, I had no idea about hair. The only thing I knew was how to go to the beauty supply store and purchase $10.99 clip-on ponytails. I knew how to brush my hair up, put a rubber band around it, slap on that little clip and then my hair was done! Hair was a subject that was the furthest from my mind, but I was willing to do my research and learn quickly once I found out the financial benefits of selling hair. I could not help but notice all the women and now some men all around the world who wear extensions. And wearing extensions is not confined to just one race. I remember growing up that girls my age were afraid to admit they were wearing extensions. But today it's a different story. It's practically a must and a definite ego-booster, and that's why this is a great business.

AM I TOO OLD TO SELL HAIR?

Not at all! I started my hair company when I was 42 years old. Please don't ever let the fear of your age stand in the way of you doing anything. We are as old as we allow ourselves to think and feel, and I don't know about you, but I turn 22 every year!

FEAR OF COMPETITION

You have to realize that hair is a billion-dollar industry. There is an abundance of wealth out there for us all to be successful. You cannot go into it with the fear of competing, because you will be limiting your growth. Competition is all around you. Look at McDonald's versus Burger King, Walgreens versus CVS, Popeye's versus KFC. These companies did not stop because of competition. This is why you have to learn how to brand yourself and make your business stand out to your customers without bashing another company. (We will get more into that in the branding section.)

NEGATIVE SUPPORT

When starting a business, you may run into people who are truly happy for you and there may be some who do not want to see you succeed. My advice is to find out who your real friends are first and then welcome their love and support. If you feel that someone around you is always doubting you, striking down all your thoughts, and telling you this and that won't work, I would strongly suggest removing them from your circle. Only surround yourself with positive people who genuinely want to see you succeed. When starting a business, who wants to hear the negative Nancies? You need all the motivation in the world, right?

FEAR OF FAILING

Let's take a look at what the word "fear" really means:

F – FALSE

E – EVIDENCE

A – APPEARING

R – REAL

We all have feelings that can be challenging from time to time. My advice is to keep going and do not look back. I find that when people do the "what if" game, they scare the crap out of themselves.

What if this does not work?

What if I lose my money?

What if I don't get any sales?

What if I can't market?

And so on, and so on.

I have always been the type of person who doesn't think too far in the future about things I don't know the answer to. I put in my mind that I will not fail and then find ways to make the impossible possible. You have to have that win mentality and the eye of the tiger. You are already starting at the bottom, so what other way can you go but up, right? You have to put it in your mind that you will have what you want to have, and do not take "no" for an answer.

Example:

You wanted to buy something on sale so bad but didn't have the money. You had a deadline to get the item before the sale ended. I'll bet anything that before the sale ended you got whatever it was you wanted, right?

Make it happen! Legally, of course.

HOW WILL YOU HANDLE BEING A BUSINESS OWNER IF YOU DON'T KNOW ANYTHING ABOUT BUSINESS?

I will tell you this: roll with the punches and everything will fall into place. I asked a lot of questions and used the web for a lot of my resources. I made sure to follow up with state laws along the way. Do not let this opportunity stop you because it is unfamiliar. You will get the hang of things. Try not to make it harder for yourself by being preoccupied with the unknown. You can be making up imaginary challenges that may never even happen.

A lot of people will turn to someone they know for advice when that person does not have any knowledge of the subject either. I would suggest getting pointers from someone who is actually doing the very thing you are wanting to do. Find out the tricks from them. I also suggest to always follow your gut feelings. We all get intuitions and hunches, and please make sure to listen to yourself. This is definitely a plug from the one above.

STAY POSITIVE

You must try to remain positive at all times. When trying something new, you cannot fill your mind with thoughts that will bring you down and scare you from pushing forward with your dreams. Stay focused and know the lifestyle you want to live is honestly up to you.

Ask~Believe~Receive

SETTING GOALS

A LITTLE INSPIRATION BEFORE LEARNING THE BUSINESS

My advice on goal setting is the following. I don't look at life the same way as most people. I teach my children to shoot for the stars while most parents will tell their children not to daydream or use their imaginations. Your imagination can take you places and cause you to think outside the box. My experience is that you want to think outside of the box because if you don't you will still be in the same box as all the other crayons. Doing the same thing. Just standing there. Be different.

I feel that no goal is too big to shoot for. You are the only one who can place limits on how far you think you should go in life. Look at the Wright brothers. They felt they would be able to fly one day. Although most people thought they were crazy and thought they would never be able to get off the ground, the brothers proved their critics wrong. You can be that next person with an idea that comes into play. Do not put limitations on how far your mind can take you. You are in control. Just think of all the self-made millionaires out there. We made our first million in sales in less than a year in business. If I had listened to others about starting a hair company, I could just be sitting at my old job right now. Take the chance.

CHAPTER TWO

LET'S TALK ABOUT HAIR

FINDING A VENDOR (MY EXPERIENCE)

When looking for a vendor, I was stumped at where to even begin. I started contacting vendor after vendor, which opened up to more and more vendors being added to my list. I started to do my research by finding a website that would tell me how long each company had been in business. We started testing out each company we came into contact with. By the time we finished, we had tested over 250 companies, of which we now use four. We sampled multiple textures and patterns from each company per order because it would save money on shipping. As you may already know, this was very costly to our company.

At the time, our experience level was brand new when it came to the hair business, so we had to do a lot of quality checking before getting enough confidence to sell it. We used close family members, friends and ourselves to test each product for perfection.

Aside from simply wearing the hair, we did strand tests, washed it and let it air dry, tried different conditioners, and bleached and colored the hair. We checked for the amount of shedding each company had, and the one thing we found out is that all hair sheds. The quality of hair and the amount of shedding is what we compared from one company to another. Once we were comfortable with a few companies we liked, we then ventured into selling to friends, co-workers and other family members at a discount.

Now we are happy to say that our hair is recognized and labeled as the best hair by most of our customers!

VENDORS WITH SECRET DISGUISES (BEWARE)

While checking quality from different companies, I found that there was a lot of deceit in the hair industry. I didn't realize that I was being contacted by many of the same companies who disguised themselves with different names. We wasted so much money not knowing we were getting the exact same hair with a different label on it. We realized this when one company we started using sent us some hair with another name and then tried to explain that it was their sister company.

If you are ever contacted by one particular company, and then three or four times in a row by others, most likely it's the same company with different names. Watch out for that.

TEST ALL HAIR BEFORE SELLING IT

Always make sure to test your hair out before selling it to your customer. Do not go based on how the hair looks through a picture or how confident a vendor sounds about their brand. Each company's job is to talk highly about their brand. It is your job to test every type of hair you would like to sell before offering it to your customers. You have to be the judge and top representative for what you are offering. You name depends on it. In our learning experience we made a horrible mistake during a sale, which cost us a bit of our reputation, but we learned our lesson and now we are fully aware of the correct process of testing out hair before selling it.

True Story:

We had the perfect representative that served our company. His customer service was the best I had ever seen. Long story short, he had an obsessive passion to one day have a cooperation with our business and his own company, instead of the company he was working for.. We were spending about $50,000 to $75,000 per week, and he made sure we had everything we needed. He left the company who was serving us and started his own. We didn't talk to him for a long time and didn't know where he went. After a while, and not knowing what had happened to him, he popped up in our email telling us the company had fired him because he had been paying too much attention to us instead of everyone else. He said how much he had missed us and told us he had started his own company and he wanted to work with us again.

We were happy he had contacted us because in a sense we had missed him too and his dedication to our company.

Well, we had a huge sale coming up for our big move into our Stockbridge, Georgia, location and we needed a massive amount of hair for this online Code Red sale and grand opening. This sale was projected to make a few hundred thousand, so we needed to make sure the stock would be there. He assured us that the quality of the hair he had was the same as we were purchasing from the other company. We had no reason not to believe him because he had worked at the other company for years. Big mistake! We trusted his word without testing first and during this major sale we found out the hard way that the quality was not the same. Do not ever sell hair you have not tested, no matter how nice the representative is. Lesson learned. That was a long time ago, but we learned from that mistake.

CUSTOMER SERVICE

GO THE EXTRA MILE

Your customer service is a huge part of your business. You must make sure the customer feels they have your direct attention and that you care about their questions and concerns. If something goes wrong, you must go the extra mile to correct any situation, especially if you caused it. Most people know you're human, and if a mistake happens, they will tend to base their forgiveness of the situation on the way you go about rectifying the problem.

Example:

You made a mistake on the customer's order and sent them something wrong. Once the customer advises you of the situation, evaluate what happened and confirm it was actually a mistake. Then make sure to apologize and take ownership of what happened. You may want to give a discount on their next order or a free item to compensate for the inconvenience.

Now that you have taken the time to fix the error and compensate the customer, this will turn the experience around to being positive. Make sure you always address your customers' concerns and do not leave them hanging. The quicker you can come up with a resolution, the better it is, and the customer will most likely return. Our motto is to always treat the customer the way we would like to be treated.

What's the first company you think of when you think of great customer service? One that comes to my mind is Chick-fil-A. I don't think I have ever been to one of their locations where their employees did not all demonstrate exceptional customer service. When running my businesses, this is the example I give to our employees as to how they should always act. I'm in the business of making sure I learn from the best and I suggest for you to pick a company to follow whose customer service has made an imprint in your mind.

RESPONDING TO NEGATIVE COMMENTS AND REVIEWS

DO NOT RESPOND WITH NEGATIVE EMOTIONS

You have to make sure if and when your company receives a negative comment or review that you are careful regarding the way you react. It can cause you more damage if you respond or reply with unhappy or angry emotions. This is where being professional really counts. Make sure to always stay in control of the conversation and remember this is your brand.

Believe us, we understand that when something untrue is said about your brand it's hard not to take it personally, especially when you have worked so hard. We suggest, when and if this arises, to take a look at what was said and to check your company to see if this is a valid complaint, and if so, use this as a way to improve. Criticism can sometimes make you see things about your company that you didn't notice. If you keep hearing the same comments from multiple people, then it's time to take a step back and evaluate what is being said.

YOU CANNOT MAKE EVERYONE HAPPY

It is impossible to make everyone happy. What one person may like another may dislike. My suggestion is to always try and please your customers to the best of your ability and within reason. The motto "The customer is always right" is what we would love to live by, but being honest, after seeing and dealing with hundreds of thousands of personalities, we have come to the conclusion that in some cases we have to agree to disagree with the customer. Your first responsibility is surely to make the customer happy, but if you find that what the customer is asking for is unrealistic, then you may have to respectfully decline what the customer wants you to do.

Example:

We had a customer come into our store with her godmother. She had been shopping with us for a while. We gave the customer a discount and a free item, showing our appreciation for her dedication to our company. Her godmother, however, did not think what we gave was enough. She wanted us to take more money off for the customer, to the point that it would have turned the transaction upside down. The customer never said anything. She was happy and loved her hair as usual. The godmother, however, did not. They left the store, and we thought the business went great. Great customer service, great hair, and a great overall experience for the customer and us. A few hours later, we received a bad review by the godmother via an app that said our customer service was horrible and we should have given more of a discount since her goddaughter shops with us all the time. This was a disappointment as well as a shock to us.

In this case, we responded respectfully and simply apologized for not being able to give additional discounts on top of the ones we had already applied.

We do not suggest responding to malicious spam, emails, or reviews that contain profanity, because they are just not worth your time. You can report those types of reviews to the company that's allowing the reviews and you can ask for comments like that to be removed.

Make time to respond to all other reviews and comments on your social media pages because customers love to engage with you. If they took the time to write to you or about you, then you may want to take the time to write a reply. We find that this builds a great relationship between you and your customers. You customer wants to know that their words make an impression on the company they chose to shop with.

MAKE SURE YOUR CUSTOMERS CAN REACH YOU

CONTACT INFORMATION

I cannot tell you how many times our customers thank us for being reachable. We have heard time and time again how hard it is for customers to reach companies by phone or email. My suggestion is to make sure your contact info is updated with your business hours, contact email, and phone number. I suggest adding the amount of time it can take you to reply to an email. Maybe give yourself 24–48 business hours. Sometimes you may miss a few calls because you are giving exceptional customer service to someone else at the time, but remember to reply to all messages. Your answering machine message should always have your business hours listed.

THERE ARE NO DUMB QUESTIONS

TAKE TIME TO EXPLAIN THE ANSWER FULLY

When your customer is asking questions, you may have been asked numerous times, remember to make sure you are taking the time to explain fully just what they're asking. This may be their first time asking a question, it may seem like a common sense question to you, it may be something you don't feel like explaining again, you may have the rules listed in full view for the customer to see, or you may feel they can find the answer or prices right on your site. Whatever the question is, take the time to answer and don't make the customer feel wrong or foolish for asking their question. When they say to you, "I know this is a dumb question," assure them that no question is a dumb question and that it is your pleasure to assist them.

WORKING WITH PARTNERS

TRUST IS IMPORTANT

When choosing a partner, make sure it's someone you can trust. When my daughter and I decided to start our businesses together there was no issue of trust whatsoever. As a matter of fact, I can work with any of my children and my sister Terri. Our business is mostly run by family members, so anyone who works for us must be able to blend in as a team and as one of the family members!

My advice is, if you're not comfortable at the thought of working with a particular person, follow your gut feeling. Sometimes money will cause strange things to happen in friendships. I personally lost a close friend because of starting a business. So, this is why I always say: keep negative people out of your circle. Surround yourself with positive people and positive vibes at all times. Surround yourself with people who are trying to make a difference in their lives. Surround yourself with people who are living a lifestyle that you want. Most importantly, choose a partner who you know will work just as hard as you or even harder to accomplish the goals you set.

With our Dropship company, we have seen multiple people break up their business relationships because one is working harder than the other. You must establish your goals before agreeing to work with each other. You must have a full understanding of what you're trying to accomplish. Each person should be responsible for certain functions, and then make sure to complete them and not leave more stress on one another.

LET'S GO DEEP INTO THE HAIR NOW

ABOUT THE HAIR

We receive many questions from people asking how the patterns are created in the hair, such as curly, deep wave, body wave, etc. We took the time to gather information directly from our vendors to ensure our answers are accurate.

Now that I'm writing a "Secrets" book, I will in fact give you the truth about the grade of the hair. I have asked my vendor with 30 years in the business to answer some of my questions so that I am able to give you the 100% truth based on the factory that produces my inventory. I have a great relationship with them, and we have always been honest with each other, so here are his answers to my questions. I did not alter his answers whatsoever. My answers come from Ted, the person I work directly with.

Q & A TIME

Ted, I am writing a book and I would like to ask you a few questions. There is a lot of information that is falsely given to customers who purchase hair, and I want to get direct answers from you. If you don't mind, please answers my questions directly and I will put your exact words in my book. Thank you so much!

Q: Where does the hair really come from?

A: *The hair is sourced from all around the world but mainly from Indian, China, and Malaysia.*

Q: How are the patterns created to ensure this is in fact virgin hair with no chemicals added?

A: *The patterns are made by steaming to ensure the patterns can last a long time.*

(We asked our other vendor this question as well to compare. She said the same thing and added that they use very high temperatures to achieve these hair patterns.)

Q: What does single and double wefted mean? Is double wefted just as it sounds? Two wefts sewn together?

A: *If the width is too wide and too difficult to wear for single weft hair, we create double weft . The double weft bundles reduce the width.*

Q: What is single drawn versus double drawn hair? What type do you sell?

A: *Double drawn means all hair lengths are the same, with no short hair. Single drawn means natural looking. We put different lengths of hair in one bundle in a reasonable percentage so the hair looks natural and not easy to tangle. What we sell is single drawn.*

Q: What is the difference between raw, virgin, and remy hair?

A: *Different customers have different understandings. In our opinion, raw hair and virgin hair are cut directly from donors, unprocessed, and all cuticles are the same direction.*

Remy hair is processed but the cuticles are still in the same direction.

(We also found out that **virgin remy hair is hair that has never been processed or chemically treated** and the cuticles are facing in one direction).

Q: Can you tell us the difference between hair grades?

Note: This is a touchy subject, but I will give you my opinion about it and then I will get to the actual answer from our vendor. When we started selling hair years ago, we sold it at 7a and 8a grades.

Healthy End

True to length
Thick bottom
No dry end
Healthy end

Exquisite Double Weft

Double weft
Strong machine weft
Tight and neat

Cuticle Hold

Bouncy and shiny
bundles with
one-direction cuticles

Our 7a was our normal hair and 8a was our highest quality at that time. Throughout the years we found that vendors gave false grades to make their customers think their hair was a higher quality than their competition.

We noticed that the hair companies started to put a spin on their products to make their quality seem higher than their competition, and then you end up with outrageous numbers such as 14a, 15a, 16a, etc.

Now granted, every year seems to get better and better—we do not doubt this—but we noticed that companies were getting ridiculous with the numbers.

Out of the four companies we purchase from, two of them are our main vendors since the beginning. When their quality changes to higher than what we currently have we then come out with a new name, such as our Tropical Line. The hair has fewer short hairs, is longer lasting, and is just really pretty. When someone asks us what our quality is, we give answers directly from our vendor shortly, but to be honest, we are happy at just saying we have premiere and premium hair and leave it at that.

Q: Can you explain the grading system in which you consider your hair to be? There are a lot of companies that will say different things and I would like to know the truth for my customers.

A: *We sell 9A (the normal you now order), 10A (high quality you use for your tropical line), and 11A and 12A is virgin hair cut directly from one head. 9A and 10A are from different donors, but customers usually sell as virgin hair too. 9A and 10A are the popular grades in the US market.*

WEIGHTS OF THE HAIR

This was not a question asked to the vendor because we knew the answers and they are pretty accurate with all the companies we purchase from as well as pretty much the same weight as most hair companies you see around.

Normal bundles range from 3.5 to 3.7 oz. although some companies will sell 5 oz. and even 7 oz. bundles. (The bigger the bundle the higher the cost.)

The following questions were asked through the years and these answers are coming from our company based on our experience and working with our vendors. I didn't want to take too much of their time by asking questions to which we knew the answers.

WHAT IS DENSITY?

The density will determine just how thick or how thin the hair is for wigs, closures and frontals mostly. Wigs will normally range between 130%, 150%, and 180%. Our top seller is 150% because it still looks very natural and not too thin or too thick. When judging the density of the closures and frontals they will normally sell at 130% for a normal look. (This is our experience with our customers and our vendors.)

HOW DO THEY GET THE #613 COLOR?

Our vendors, along with most vendors, bleach the hair at a high temperature to get the desired look of #613. To actually get blonde hair that grows directly from the scalp is possible, but the cost of the hair will be so high that it will be hard to resell, based on our experience and price checking. The blonde hair we sell is a very high quality. Our second vendor is who we obtain this hair from. They told us the high quality of blonde that we purchase is only bought by us and one other company. Otherwise, they sell a lower quality to the rest of their customers for a lower cost.

THE TRUTH ABOUT SHEDDING HAIR

While asking questions to our vendors we have come to find out the truth about shedding hair. Although all companies would like to say their hair does not shed, this is far from the truth. All hair sheds, just as your own hair will shed, especially curly and wavy textures. The difference is normal shedding and excessive shedding—which is what a customer will not tolerate. Most of the time the normal shedding will come from the machine not catching all of the hair strands when they are in the sewing process. You may end up with a few loose hairs and this is normal. Typically, once you run your hands through it a few times that will take care of hairs that the machine didn't catch.

If you continuously get a large amount of hair that sheds, this may be a serious problem. I would advise you to have a serious discussion with your vendor. If nothing changes, then seek another vendor. That kind of shedding would not be tolerated by us or your customers.

TYPES OF LACE

Although there are quite a few types of lace, I am going to list the most common ones and what we sell. Out of all the years we've been selling hair, we have only been asked a handful of times about the type of lace we sell. To be honest, we were selling hair a few years in before the question even came up.

SILK LACE

The base of the closures and the frontals are silk. Customers like silk bases because the knots are not seen, and it appears more natural and looks like the hair is coming directly from the scalp.

SWISS LACE VERSUS FRENCH LACE

French lace has smaller holes, therefore there is more hair and the hair is thicker and more durable. However, Swiss lace has bigger holes with less hair but gives a very natural hair line and is more commonly sold. If you're new to having frontals and closures, you may want French lace if the company sells it, only because you have more room for error. The only thing is, you may have to do a bit more plucking for the hairline to look natural. Most companies offer pre-plucked options. (Our closures and frontals come pre-plucked.) If your wig is made from French lace it will be more durable for combing and tugging. The Swiss is for a more experienced customer and is more preferred because of the natural look it gives. (We primarily sell Swiss Lace.)

TRANSPARENT, 3D FILM, AND ILLUSION LACE

When these names came out we were a bit confused. They seemed the same but were called different names, so we checked with our vendors and they all agreed that these are all the same type of lace. The lace is see-through for all three, so the hairs will look like they are coming directly from your scalp.

PRE-PLUCKED CLOSURES AND FRONTALS

If you ask the company if the closures and frontals are pre-plucked and they say yes, this means it has a more natural hair line. A natural hairline is not very thick at the base so they will pluck some hairs to thin it out a bit.

(Ours are considered pre-plucked.) Even if the company tells you the closure or frontal is pre-plucked, you most likely have to do some work based on your hairline to match up the lace perfectly.

TYPES OF WIGS

There are three wig types that are requested from our company the most.

Full Lace—This means the entire inside of the cap is fully lace based. You will be able to part your hair just as your own natural hair with no restrictions.

Lace Front—This means that the front of the hairline from ear to ear is 13 inches across and depending on the company we use to purchase the wig from, it may go from the forehead back 3 inches or 6 inches. The remainder of the wig is sewn with weft extensions.

360 Frontal Wig—This wig will have lace all around the entire circumference of the head. You will be able to easily pull it up in a ponytail as well as part it all around. The top center of the wig will be track hair.

If styled correctly, it will be hard to tell which wig type you're actually wearing.

CHAPTER THREE

HAIR CARE

This is a very important subject, simply because if the customer does not know the proper care for their hair products then it can determine their overall experience with your company. We found that giving them hair care tips based on our experience working with each type of hair will help ensure a pleasant experience and a positive review for your company.

We are not licensed cosmetologists, but we do know how our hair reacts based on our customers as well as us wearing the hair. We advised you to check with a professional stylist for expert tips or we will give you our feedback based on our experience working with this type of hair. Below are our suggestions for hair care.

CO-WASH THE HAIR WHEN YOU FIRST GET IT

Surprisingly, a lot of people do not co-wash their hair when they first get it. This is something that I always suggest you do. Although our hair ships quickly from our warehouse and it does not sit long with us, we cannot tell you what happens to it before it's imported across country to us. We cannot guarantee how long it is held where it is before orders are shipped to us.

CURLY TEXTURE ROUTINES

Now my opinion and advice on this type of hair is pretty great, since I have been dealing with this myself for 46 years so far. My hair is naturally curly and resembles our Indian curly hair to be exact. My hair is considered to be 3B-3C type hair. I can surely tell you curly hair is gorgeous, but the way you go to sleep at night will NOT be the way you wake up in the morning. You may look like a chia pet! So, with this being said, curly hair is a bit on the higher maintenance side, but if you follow my suggestions this can be the most exotic look for you!

You must explain to your customers when dealing with this type of hair that water and conditioner will be their best friends. They will need to saturate the hair with water and apply some type of curly lotion of their choice or just simply add conditioner with water into a warm spray bottle and use that. After wetting their hair, they will need to go through it with a wig brush (I actually use the plastic kinds because it really makes my hair pop!). Once they are done styling the hair, just make sure they know to **LEAVE THE HAIR ALONE! DO NOT FINGER THROUGH THE HAIR!** Once it's dry, it's okay to shake the curls to fluff them up but do not finger through, because this will distort and frizz your curls.

I will give you the actual product I use on my hair. It smells and reacts the best with curls, in my opinion from all the products I've tried so far. I'm continuously getting compliments on my curls and questions on how I maintain my curls all day. When walking past people, they always tell me how good my hair smells. Here is a picture. I hope you love this product like I do.

(*A little trick*: When naturally drying your hair, use a cotton T-shirt or microfiber towels to absorb the water. I have found that towels will cause a lot of frizz.)

DEEP WAVE TEXTURE

I would follow the exact same directions I mentioned above if you would like to wear it in its natural curly or wavy texture.

BODY WAVE AND STRAIGHT

This hair is the easiest hair to maintain. You will simply style as desired. But what I have learned from dealing with certain stylists is that if you straighten your hair one day and the next day you decide to wear it with curls or waves using curling irons, you may want to completely wash your hair, condition, and blow-dry before applying your desired curls. Doing this will allow your hair to reset and hold the curls all day. If you try to curl it right after wearing it completely bone straight you may run into issues with the hair not holding the curls because it has been molded with the flat iron for straightness. I found this to be true after trying this myself. Once again, I'm no professional. This is just based on asking questions as well as experience.

LOOSE WAVE

Now this is the most versatile hair ever in my opinion. The reason I say this is because you can wear this hair in its natural waves by doing the curly techniques and you will see this hair with the most gorgeous roller coaster waves. You can also use the techniques for straight and body wave. (Just remember my advice when switching up the styles by washing, conditioning, and blow drying, especially if you have worn the hair naturally and put a product on it and now you want to change it to straight or desired curls. You will want to wash the product out.)

BLEACHING FRONTALS, CLOSURES, AND WIGS

PROS AND CONS

There is a good and bad effect when bleaching frontals, closures and wigs. This is something that is done to create a natural look and remove the black dots on the scalp area of the lace. When this is done correctly, the desired outcome is to look like the hair is growing directly out of your scalp. Most people will in fact take this chance for a perfect look.

The bad part is that if this is not done correctly you will damage the lace. Just think about it—this is a thin piece of lace. The strands of hair are embedded with a single knot only. If you leave the bleach on it too long, or you do not wash the bleach out completely, it will continue to bleach. The bleach with then eat at the lace, which will destroy the lace and ultimately cause your product to shed tremendously. We do not suggest that anyone do this, so we will not give our opinions on how to accomplish this look. We do suggest people use concealer of their natural color to get their desired results. This will allow a longer lasting frontal, closure or wig.

CLOSING OF HAIR CARE

Just remember the products you sell will be a definite reflection of your company. Your customers' choice to continue to shop with you will be determined by a few major factors.

YOUR PRODUCT

Make sure to always sell the best products you can find. Remember, what one likes another may not like, so when determining if your products are great, then judge that based on the percentage of people who are giving positive feedback. If you're gaining more negative feedback versus positive, then a change needs to be made.

CUSTOMER SERVICE

Make sure you're going the extra mile to show appreciation to your customers for shopping with you. Make them feel like family and always make the customer know they are appreciated. For situations where you know you can easily rectify a problem, then do your very best to make the customer happy. Customers want to know they mean something to the company they choose to shop with. Remember, they can shop with plenty of other companies, but they chose you! Without your customers you have no company.

GRATITUDE

Give gratitude daily for all your accomplishments and success. This is food for the soul, and it keeps you grounded and reminds you of what life could have been like if you hadn't taken the first step of starting your own business. Always show appreciation to the one above for making this happen.

CHAPTER FOUR

NOW THAT WE KNOW ABOUT THE HAIR, LET'S GET TO BUSINESS!

You have no idea how much you have accomplished by simply making a decision to start your own hair company. I found out throughout the years just by talking to people that most do not know what they want to do in life. Be proud of yourself because you have taken a step toward making a change and living the lifestyle of your dreams!

BRANDING

When deciding the type of hair company you wish to own and represent, I personally feel you must stand out from the rest. When we decided to start Boss Xtend, my main concern was to not duplicate the same looks I saw in every other hair company. I felt there was too much glitter, sparkles, and pink colors everywhere. Although it's a great look and its popular, I wanted to show more of a dominant and "Boss" look. We chose the colors black and red because we felt this would be a more powerful image. (I feel we made the right decision based on our customers.)

My advice is to sit and think hard on how you can be different than the rest of your competition. What makes your company stand out? Why should people purchase from you? What do you do differently than the rest? These are some things to think about.

NAMING YOUR COMPANY

This is another part of your branding and what makes you stand out from the rest. You may just want to name your company based on meaningful things like your name. You may want to name it after someone meaningful in your life, but powerful names sometimes attract customers first because of the name's appeal. I have purchased items from stores based on the names alone because it made me feel like they described my personality when they came up with the name. It gave me a positive impression.

My suggestion is to look to your inner self and ask the question, what is the best name for my company? What do I want my name to represent? What impression do I want to give to my customers? How can I be different from the rest? Do it before you go to bed and you may just be surprised if you have the name by morning. It will come to you. My personal advice is to just be different than the rest. Create your own image and don't blend it with other companies. Stand out!

LOGO

You may already have an idea of an image to represent your hair company or you may have absolutely no idea. My opinion is the same as naming your company. Think about it before you go to bed. Come up with the colors you like. Try sketching out a few ideas and don't worry about the result—you don't have to be an expert. Most of the time you can give the person designing your logo a couple of ideas and you will be surprised how they can come up with the perfect logo for you.

PACKAGING

Once you come up with the perfect name, colors, and logo, it will be time for you to seek packaging. When deciding your type of packaging, I want you to keep something in mind. Make sure this packaging is cost-effective for you. While working with a lot of hair companies with our Dropship program, we had some companies send us huge boxes to pack their orders, but we had to tell them the size of the boxes will incur an extra charge to ship. The post office and FedEx will surely charge a lot of money to ship these big items and you will then have to charge a lot for your shipping to cover this box. Your customer will then say your shipping is too high.

If you must have big packaging, you can always include it in the cost of your bundles, but still, you are taking a risk for your pricing. My advice is to come up with a look that can fit inside of the USPS priority padded pack.

Some companies will send us neck wraps, tags, bows, box types, hair cards, stickers, ribbons, bags, etc. As long as it can fit in the packaging, it won't be costly to ship your products.

Once again, make it cute, and make it stand out, because when getting reviews, for example, on YouTube, it makes an impression on your customers. It makes you feel great to see them pull out your packaging and make positive comments to their viewers. Take your time and be creative!

WEBSITES AND WEB HOSTING

DOMAIN NAMES

There are plenty of companies you can purchase a domain name from. I use GoDaddy for all my accounts.

Be creative when selecting a domain name. The goal is to choose the same name as your company, but sometimes this won't work out the way you planned. I feel you should try to get the one that ends with .com instead of ones like .net, .co, etc. The .com is looked at to be more dominant. If you find that your name is not available, then you will be faced with a few decisions, like changing your business name slightly to be evenly matched with your domain name or vice versa.

DOMAIN EXPIRATION DATES

Make sure you keep up with the dates your domain names will expire, because if you let them go without renewing them someone can take your domain name if it's up for sale. You do not want this to happen, especially after being in business for a while. I suggest you purchase at least two years at first. Domains are fairly inexpensive.

Be aware of the many offers the companies will try to upsell you with during your checkout process. They may offer you to pay longer terms, privacy protections, purchase emails, etc. Be careful when clicking boxes during the checkout. You may just be purchasing something you don't really need.

WEB HOSTING

Now it's time for you to get a website. There are a lot of companies you can obtain your sites from. Here is a list of reputable companies. The ones I listed here are known to be user friendly.

Shopify.com (This is who we use.)

Wix.com

GoDaddy.com

Squarespace.com

Web.com

Website.com

Weebly.com

BUILDING YOUR WEBSITE

This is your opportunity to show off your products. Here are a few subjects and fields you want to cover to make your customers interested what you have to offer.

Pictures of all your products

Great sales and deals on your products

Sliders (the big pictures that change across the top of the site)

About us

Terms and conditions

Shipping

Contact info

Payment providers (PayPal, Stripe, etc.)

Social media links

Logo (optional at first but highly suggested at some point)

Anything else you would like your customers to know

Reviews

Quick links

Your website is an extension of your brand. When building the site make sure you do it with love. My suggestion is to think about what you like to see when you search a site. Make sure the navigation is easy and products are easy to locate. Try your best to make this site stand out from the rest.

APPS

You will find many apps that can help you increase your sales. My suggestion is to make sure you at least have an email collector app. You will want to be able to acquire your own marketing list so that you're able to send out your sale deals to your potential buyers. The great advantage with Shopify as your website host is that they have tons of useful apps to use.

CHAPTER FIVE

LET'S MAKE SOME MONEY!

In this section I will share with you my secrets when it comes to the most important part of your business – making a profit. Through the years I have learned customers are always looking for a great deal. (Who doesn't want a great deal?) They want to get the most for their money.

We searched over 250 companies since we started to the present day to try and find the perfect quality hair. It was also important to get the best quality and the best price so that we could offer our customers high quality hair for less.

We came up with a special sale that we are known for called "Code Red." During this sale I get really creative, finding ways to give a lot of hair options for a very low cost. I would suggest that you come up with a cool sale type that can be a part of your branding and something your customers will get excited to see happening. I would suggest that you do this sale maybe every six months or come up with a time frame that's best for you.

TYPES OF SALES

Here is where it gets fun. You definitely want to look at your competition and get ideas of what they are doing or what they have done in the past so that you can stay on top of what's trending. For me, I always try to figure out a way I can attract the customer by giving much more than my competition.

Here are examples of types of sales I found that works for us.

2 Bundles + Closure

2 Bundles + Frontal

2 Bundles + 360 Frontal

Buy 2 Bundles Get a Free Bundle

Buy 2 Bundles Get a Free Closure

Buy 3 Bundles Get a Free Frontal

#613 Hair Sales

Full Lace Wig Sale

Frontal Wig Sale

Bogo Deals

Bestie Deals (Boss Xtend created—you may want to rename)

These are top sellers for us. Now remember, I'm going based on our sales and what works for us so try these top sellers that I suggested and also come up with new ones to try out. You basically just want to keep any ideas that work for you and throw away the rest!

HOW TO PRICE YOUR HAIR

When pricing your hair, I think that some people tend to get a bit greedy and this is why things don't go as planned. Now if pricing highly is working for you, then by all means keep it going! If it's not working for you, my suggestion is to go a bit lower than normal, especially in the beginning while trying to establish a name for yourself. If you price your hair low, it will attract more people and you will make so much more in volume. The average person who comes across a great hair sale will then tell their friends and family.

When I'm having a sale, I will focus on how much I want to make off the deal itself rather than focus on the amount off each bundle. Some will try to make over $50 off each bundle, then by the time the person gets what they need for a full head they have paid way too much. So, determine the ideal amount you would like to make from each person and start there.

EXAMPLES

Here are a few ideas you can use. These price examples are based off our current Dropship prices. If you have your own vendors, then adjust your sales according to the cost of your inventory.

BUNDLES

Brazil Hair Per Bundle

COST	SALE PRICE	PROFIT
10" - $29	$50 - $70+	$22 - $42+
12" - $35	$55 - $70+	$20 - $35+
14" - $37	$60 - $75+	$23 - $38+
16" - $41	$65 - $80+	$22 - $42+
18" - $45	$70 - $85+	$27 - $42+
20" - $46	$75 - $90+	$29 - $44+
22" - $50	$80 - $95+	$31 - $46+
24" - $54	$85 - $100+	$32 - $47+
26" - $58	$90 - $105+	$32 - $47+
28" - $63	$95 - $110+	$32 - $47+
30" - $68	$100 - $115+	$32 - $47+

Mink Hair Per Bundle

COST	SALE PRICE	PROFIT
10" - $29	$51 - $70+	$22 - $42+
12" - $35	$55 - $70+	$20 - $35+
14" - $37	$60 - $75+	$23 - $38+
16" - $41	$65 - $80+	$22 - $42+
18" - $45	$70 - $85+	$27 - $42+
20" - $46	$75 - $90+	$29 - $44+
22" - $50	$80 - $95+	$31 - $46+
24" - $54	$85 - $100+	$32 - $47+
26" - $58	$90 - $105+	$32 - $47+
28" - $63	$95 - $110+	$32 - $47+
30" - $68	$100 - $115+	$32 - $47+

When it comes to other textures, you can follow the same suggested prices above.

BUNDLE DEAL SUGGESTIONS

Brazil Hair Bundle Deals Subtracting $15

PRICE	COST
10"-$60	$29
12"-$65	$35
14"-$70	$37
16"-$75	$41
18"-$80	$45
20"-$85	$46
22"-$90	$50
24"-$95	$54
26"-$100	$58
28"-$105	$63
30"-$110	$68

DEAL	DISCOUNT	COST	PROFIT
10-12-14 = $195	-$15		$79
12-14-16 = $210	-$15		$82
14-16-18 = $225	-$15		$87
16-18-20 = $240	-$15		$93
18-20-22 = $255	-$15		$99
20-22-24 = $270	-$15		$105
22-24-26 = $285	-$15		$122
24-26-28 = $300	-$15		$110
26-28-30 = $315	-$15		$111
28-30-30 = $325	-$15		$111

(TOP SELLERS / -COST)

The bundle deal example chart above explains how you can construct your actual bundle deals. Use this as a guideline when creating your deals. You can either make them a bit higher or a bit lower, it just depends on you.

On the left side I made the example as if you chose these particular prices for each bundle. Next will be the cost that you pay your vendor (hopefully it's us). The section that follows will show a bundle deal example. Feel free to get creative. Next you will see the -$15 discount. Lastly, you deduct the cost of each bundle and you will end up with your profits on the right.

The section that is highlighted within the bundle deals lets you know that these are top sellers. So, if you look to the right of the top sellers you will see your profits look great!

When creating bundle deals, I always concentrate on how much I will make from the deal versus the amount I make off each bundle. I feel this is where most people make mistakes and are not as successful as they would like to be with their sales. If you make the prices too high, then it is not a sale, right? I would suggest making your bundle discounts to be within $15 to $20 off the normal purchase price. The lower your bundle deals are, the more attractive your company is to your customers.

LOSE A LITTLE TO GAIN A LOT

Sometimes you may have to give away a little more than you would like to in order to gain a lot more in return. Customers love to get free products, so if you do deals that consist of free closures, free frontals, and free bundles this will be a great eye catcher! I would not suggest applying a bundle deal discount on top of a free item deal. When giving away free items, I would suggest charging full price for the hair and then really give the chosen item away free.

Some companies will try to charge more, and the customers may sometimes think this is some kind of gimmick. So be honest and really give the items away for free. You will notice that word of mouth will spread really quickly on free item deals!

FREE CLOSURE DEALS

Brazil Hair Bundle Deals Subtracting $15

PRICE	COST		DEAL	DISCOUNT	COST	PROFIT
10"-$60	$29					
12"-$65	$35					
14"-$70	$37		10-12-14 = $195	-$15		$79
16"-$75	$41		12-14-16 = $210	-$15		$82
18"-$80	$45		14-16-18 = $225	-$15		$87
20"-$85	$46		16-18-20 = $240	-$15	-COST	$93
22"-$90	$50		18-20-22 = $255	-$15		$99
24"-$95	$54		20-22-24 = $270	-$15		$105
26"-$100	$58		22-24-26 = $285	-$15		$122
28"-$105	$63		24-26-28 = $300	-$15		$110
30"-$110	$68		26-28-30 = $315	-$15		$111
			28-30-30 = $325	-$15		$111

You are able to use this same guideline when doing free bundles and other discounts too! We suggest you research other hair companies and see what they are selling their products for, then use your guidelines in pricing. We suggest that you to stay within the selling range, especially when you're just starting off.

Play around with your numbers and see what you can come up with. This part, adding up your potential earnings, is actually pretty fun.

HOLIDAYS AND CUSTOMER APPRECIATION SALES

Most people surely count on companies having some sort of holiday or customer appreciation sales. Make sure you're prepared and aware of what holidays are coming up so that you can plan accordingly. Design your flyers according to the holiday or special deal at hand.

CHAPTER SIX

MARKETING

Marketing is not just a small part of owning a successful hair company—it is the backbone of your entire business. If you don't let everyone know your business is active then they won't be in the market for purchasing your products, right? This is extremely critical to the sales of your company. If you have no sales then you have no company.

TOP FIVE REASONS MARKETING IS IMPORTANT

1. Marketing grows business

2. Marketing notifies your potential customers

3. Marketing builds branding for your company

4. Marketing increases website traffic for 24-hour online purchases

5. Marketing increases your company's credibility

HOW TO ADVERTISE YOUR COMPANY

SOCIAL MEDIA PLATFORMS

When you look at businesses back in the day, they simply had to rely on word of mouth to the spread the existence of their companies. People would either give a great review and tell all their friends and family about the business or they would give a negative review, but nevertheless, the word of mouth was key. Nowadays it's so much easier to spread news about your business since we have great social media platforms.

I have looked at some statistics involving social media trends and educated myself on the fact that as of 2018, there are more than three billion people using social media platforms per month. Needless to say, exposing your business with this type of marketing is a must!

INSTAGRAM

For our company, Instagram has been our leading avenue of marketing. We use Shopify and it tells us through our reports where our sales come from primarily and we were blown away at the amount of traffic that comes in from that platform.

Instagram will allow you to create a business page and profile for your company. With this option you will be able to run ads and promotions, but you must have a Facebook page to use this marketing tool.

You will be able to set up a budget, choose a target audience, target area, post an ad and publish.

We have found that using the proper hash tags when posting your pictures on your page will bring in leads as well.

YOUTUBE

If you have been following us, then I cannot express to you how YouTube has been such an extremely powerful marketing tool for our business. My daughter Sparkle Marie has made a great impression on our customers by displaying our products on YouTube. She uses this avenue to engage with our potential customers by showing them just how beautiful the hair is in motion. She is able to answer questions and show the varieties of hair we sell.

If you have someone who will be able to market using YouTube as one of your primary sources this will help to boost your sales tremendously. Make sure you're using the "How to" titles to attract your customers to your channel.

Other social media platforms that are helpful in the increase of your sales are:

Facebook

Twitter

Snapchat

WhatsApp

Tumblr

Pinterest

LinkedIn

There are many social media platforms and apps continuously being created to expand your business. Please make sure you're using these features to help brand your business. This will be a key factor in the success of your brand.

GIVE-A-WAYS AND CONTESTS

Customers love free items. When they see give-a-ways this will surely attract them to your page. Display the product and have them do different activities to qualify them to enter. You can have them do things such as spread the word about your business by having them tag 20 people. Have these 20 people follow you on your social media pages. You can tell them to state why they should be the winner. Once you find the qualifications that will qualify the contestant to win your contest, make sure you post them as the winner and a picture of them using your product they won.

OFFER COUPONS

Offering coupon codes when placing orders is another great tool in assisting your leads to make the actual purchase. We have it set up on our website that once a person looks at our products and adds items into their cart, they will receive an email that will offer them a discount code to use to make the item more attractive to purchase. This feature is for abandoned carts.

Offering different discount codes on social media platforms will also give you an idea where your sales are coming from. You can use a different one for each platform if you like if you want to keep records for yourself.

BRAND AMBASSADORS

When starting a hair company, it is a good idea to have some brand ambassadors. You will need to have pictures to match the type of hair you're selling. You can either give your brand ambassadors free hair to promote or you can give them a great discount in return for the pictures and posts to their sites.

You will want to find brand ambassadors that have large followings so that when they post pictures many will see what you have to offer. It will have to be worthwhile to you, especially if you're giving free hair to this person and in return they're showing it to a large number of potential customers.

You can assign a code to your brand ambassadors and when the customer uses their code it will give the customer $5 to $10 off the product. You will then know if it is worth it to give the particular ambassador free hair or not. If they are bringing in plenty customers than it is surely worth it! If not, thank them for their time and find others. Make sure to always be respectful and appreciative to your ambassadors because they can get you good and bad feedback. You're only wanting the good!

A little warning: while selling hair you will get tons of messages from people who would love to be your brand ambassadors. So, make sure to research these potential prospects to ensure they will be a good fit for your company. You will have to make sure they will meet all the qualifications that you require in a brand ambassador.

QUALITY OF PHOTOS

Make sure you're posting great quality pictures. You will have to make sure you and your brand ambassadors are posting clear, well lit, full-hair pics, and no emojis and heavy filters. This is very critical to the sales of your products.

The customers want to see what the hair really looks like. Misrepresentation of your hair will lead you to nothing but headaches and complaints.

HANDING OUT FLYERS AND HAIR CARDS

This is a great way to promote your company. Hand out at least 100 flyers or hair cards and by the end of the week look how many people you have contacted. Imagine the potential customers telling at least one person they know about your products, and now you have doubled the amount of potential buyers.

Make sure your hair is done when handing out your flyers. I cannot express to you how much of an impression this gives your customers about your company. If they see that your hair is gorgeous, then they will want that same look. If your hair is looking a mess, then nine times out of ten the flyer is going in the garbage. So, make an impression when handing out the cards.

My daughter Sparkle Marie flew into many cities handing out the hair cards while making sure her hair was flawless. She had her makeup on, nice clothes and just gave the total look that most want to achieve. To be honest, she was a walking, live billboard and a total representation of what we had to offer the customer. So, make sure you're making an impression, and remember, no one will work as hard for your company as you do!

EMAIL COLLECTOR APPS

Collecting emails is a big part your online marketing as well. Using these apps will enable you to build relationships with your customers, potential customers, prospects and subscribers.

The emails you generate will enable you to engage directly with your customers, letting them know of discounts, sales, new products and what's new with your hair company.

You can build your email list by using the email collector apps. Most apps come with creative and fun ways for a customer to input their emails. They even have ones that consist of games to play that will ultimately give the customer discounts toward a purchase once they input their email.

EMAIL MARKETING COMPANIES

Using an email marketing company will save you so much time. Imagine yourself having to email each customer one by one to tell them of the exciting new things happening with your company. This will take so much of your time.

Signing up for an email marketing company will allow you to upload all your emails into files within the site. You can separate customers into groups and send advertisements accordingly. You may have customers who only love to wear blonde hair, who love bundle deals, who wear long lengths, etc. Making separate groups and sending them information they are interested in will be more effective in the long run.

Ultimately, you want to let everyone know everything, but you may have certain groups you want to send specials to.

This is also a way you can separate exclusive offers for certain customers via a loyalty program. You may want to send them extra discounts and extra appreciation emails. You may want to run a sale just for your VIP customers. You can become very creative on finding reasons to separate groups and also just sending out important information involving your brand.

There are plenty of email marketing companies, but I use Constant Contact. I have never had any issues with them, and their customer service is amazing. Take the time to do research and see which company is right for you.

GOSSIP CHANNEL ADS

Most people are very interested in gossip. People want to see what's going on inside another's world and because of the need to know, they have created gossip sites on social media. This is a perfect way to advertise your business. They will charge you a fee but the returns most of the time make it well worth it.

When choosing to advertise on such platforms as the gossip sites, I recommend that you have tough skin. These channels seek attention and the people who are making comments also seek attention. Just understand that people will have their negative comments, but you will gain business from the ones who are interested during the process.

INTEGRITY

I felt I should bring this subject up because its sets the foundation of your company. You want to always make sure you're giving honest information to your customers to the best of your ability. If there is something you don't know check it out first. People want to know they are shopping with a good, reputable company that has morals. Do not get into just telling them what they want to hear to make the sale.

POSTING CONTENT ON YOUR SOCIAL MEDIA

Make sure you're posting your customers' pictures—approved pictures, and not pictures you have no rights to use. I think it's helpful when posting your customers to tag them in the pictures. This will allow any potential customer to be able to ask that person questions as well as let them know this is actually your customer. There are too many companies who will steal other hair company's pictures and use them falsely as their own.

If you take part in this misrepresentation, you will build an unwanted and untrustworthy negative image of your company. You don't want this.

WHAT CAN I POST IF I DON'T HAVE ANY CONTENT?

Everyone starts here, and believe me, it's a rough spot. If you don't have any content it's hard to get anyone to purchase from you, right? So, what do you do? You will have to take a lot of pictures of yourself, your family, your friends, and "get the look" pictures.

A lot of companies will post pictures of celebrity hair types. If you choose to do this then please make sure to add "get the look" and the fact that this is not your hair, but they can achieve this same look using your hair and then list the type of hair that will match the look. This is the most honest way to fill up your page with content until your pictures start flooding in. Remember to offer some of your customers discounts in return for their photos to post on your social media. We all started here when it comes to hair companies, so no worries, you will get past this! I just want you to do it the right way.

OVERCOMING SABOTAGE

BEWARE

When we decided to sell hair, we immediately agreed that we wanted to be a company who gave high quality hair for less. This strategy we started was not liked by a lot of our competitors and we started to notice a lot of negative actions being done against our company. We had other companies target our customers and tell them false things about us while trying to direct the customer to another company (most likely their own) to purchase hair. We have been told numerous amounts of time by our customers that they were contacted by so many people trying to get them to shop elsewhere, but because of the dedication our customers have with us they delete their invites and ignore the foolish attempts to take our customers away from us. Below is an actual message sent to our customers from another hair company

"I wouldn't recommend boss Xtend.She never gave me a refund and deleted all my comments. I hate to have to stop the flow of a young black entrepreneur, but I have to do what's right for the people and that's to inform you on the hair. They only give their best hair to

selected customers. Wish you the best, sorry to inform you on this. If you ever need to know where to get great hair from just dm me."

We had another one just like this going around from another major hair company who we chose not to mention in this book. In that message they actually said which hair company to go and shop with along with the fact they had discount codes to use.

We had a young lady tell us when she was in the hospital her nurse sold hair and our customer told the nurse she was faithful to us. Our customer told us the nurse offered to pay her to discredit our company. When I heard this, I was shocked. We know there are other hair companies that have people make bad reviews and comments on videos, but to offer to pay someone to talk bad about us is crazy to me.

We believe in *Karma* bigtime, so we are not bothered by this type of nonsense. We have made mistakes in the past during our learning period and we are human. It happens. We took our mistakes and learned from them to bring our customers the best hair for less and we will continue to do so.

CHAPTER SEVEN

YOUR IMAGE

Do not get into bashing other companies. Do not make comments on other hair page pictures. Do not disrespect other hair companies with advertising under their paid ads. This is done to us all the time. But guess what? There is a rule in the universe that like attracts like. What you do to others will be done to you. Doing this will only cause you the same problems.

There is a fair way of telling people you know are in the market for hair about your company. When you know there is a certain group of people in the market of purchasing hair, it is okay to contact them in their personal inbox and invite them to look at what you have to offer, but it is not okay to discredit another company.

Bad Example:

This hair company has trash hair and you should shop with me.

Good Example:

Hello, I see you're in the market for hair. I just wanted to introduce my company to you and maybe one day I will have an opportunity to tell you about my products. If you have any questions, feel free to let me know. Enjoy your day!

There is definitely etiquette on how to advertise your business. Do not sabotage another company—that's just not professional. Do not use another company as hashtags on your ads. When other customers hashtag (#) a particular company to see what they have available and your ad comes up, to me that's just horrible. This is my opinion. It's okay to hashtag the types of businesses that may have customers interested in your products, but just not a particular company.

Good Example:

#newyorksalons #nychair #brazilianbundles #straightbundles #hairsales #LAhair #tapehair #clipinhair

Do not advertise your business using someone else's advertisements. We are saying this because, for example, we advertise on theshaderoom. com, but when these ads post almost all the time you will see other hair companies make comments under the ads telling customers to shop with them. This is very tacky and distasteful. If we take the time to pay Shade Room $2,500, or whatever the price is to run our ads and videos, I don't feel it's right for another company to promote their brand using our advertisement. This will make you angry too, right?

Stay positive, treat other companies with respect, and the doors of opportunity and sales will come flooding in. There is enough for all of us to be successful out here without stepping on anyone else's toes. We all can be successful if we go about it the right way—with integrity.

PROCEED WITH CAUTION

You will have to be very careful when orders start to come in. Unfortunately, not everyone is honest, and you may find that you will be tested for the security of your orders.

FRAUDULENT ORDERS AND CHARGEBACKS

When it comes to online shopping, you have to be careful of the orders coming into your web store. If there is an order that you don't feel comfortable fulfilling, then cancel and refund it.

In the beginning when you first start obtaining sales you will be excited, and who wants to think that someone can be trying to get one over on you? This is not a good feeling. We lost so much money when we first started, not knowing the fraud attempts that were out there. We never committed any fraud, so we never thought anyone would do it to us.

We ended up fulfilling countless orders and then finding out the funds were taken away from us. Our hearts dropped and the feeling of quitting did come to mind. We picked ourselves up and understood that there was just a lot of negativity around and we would have to learn how to protect ourselves and our products.

It's hard to at first get extremely excited that you have a sale, send out the order, then shortly after receive information that money has been taken out of your account and returned to the credit card holder, finding out your sale was fraudulent and now not having any way getting your products back. That sucks!

Learn how to identify fraudulent orders and also make sure to use the fraud filters that come with the website apps. I recommend that for large orders that have one name and address as the biller and another name and address as the shipping and are going to different states, you may want to do some type of security check before sending.

Shopify comes with a fraud filter that will tell you if there are risks detected before filling the orders. They will give you alerts as to it being normal, medium risk, or high risk. We cancel any orders that come with high risk and we ask for documents confirming identity for the medium risks and orders with addresses that don't match.

SIGNS OF FRUADULENT ORDERS

1. Large orders and long lengths

2. Rush orders/mandatory overnight needed

3. Several transaction attempts

4. Billing and shipping addresses not matching

5. Multiple orders being placed from the same IP address using different cards

6. Medium to high risk alerts

7. Using fake phone numbers and fake emails

8. There are third-party companies you can hire for this as well but if the sale does not feel right to you, I would suggest canceling and refunding. Don't take any chances.

CUSTOMERS CLAIMS OF NOT GETTING THEIR ORDERS

This is something you don't want to think of, but it does happen. Not all of these claims are true. Every so often we are tested to see if we will send out another order.

We suggest that if this happens to you, please make sure to tell the customer to give you a police report as well as a claim with the post office and make sure you follow up on this information. You will be amazed at how many packages are instantly located once you inform the customer that the police will be involved. The neighbor had it, my dad had it, it was in my mailbox, etc.

ADD SIGNATURES ON EVERY ORDER

We suggest that on every order you send out make sure that the person has to sign for it. This adds extra security to your packages and cuts down a lot of the false claims about not getting their package when someone has clearly signed for it at their address.

TERMS AND CONDITIONS

COMPANY POLICIES

You want to make sure your customers are well aware of your policies. Not every company operates the same way, so make sure you're clear as to what the customer should expect when ordering hair from you.

Do you offer returns?

Do you offer refunds?

Do you offer credits?

Shipping policy

Et cetera

Make sure you take your time and try not to leave anything out, because your customer will come up with unexpected situations and attempts that you will need to have a policy in place to uphold.

MISTAKES HAPPEN

YOU ARE HUMAN

As much as you try to be on top of everything that is going on, we as humans do make mistakes. Learn to recover from your mistakes on a positive note, learn from the error, and try to be better the next time. If you are at fault, then offer the customer some type of compensation and a sincere apology. Always come up with new strategies to rectify the problem at hand and work for solutions to catch the errors before shipping the items to your customers.

Good luck with your ventures!

CHAPTER EIGHT

CLOSING

You have taken the first step in changing your life. Make sure to keep negative people out of your circle. Surround yourself with people who will influence you to live to the best of your ability.

Understand that your personal success is judged only by you. What may be labeled as success to someone may not be success to another. This is about you and your life. This is about what's important to you. It may not matter about the money or the fame. What are your dreams? What makes you happy? What makes you feel complete? Whatever you choose, just be the best at it.

Give gratitude daily for what you already have and remember there are no limits to what you can achieve in life. You're the only one who can set the limits for your life.

~ Dalandra Young

ABOUT THE AUTHOR

In 2014 my daughter and I decided to take a leap of faith and start a hair company not knowing the first thing about hair. We had no idea our venture would take us where we are today.

My daughter and I worked for Delta Airlines at the time. She had about two years of experience and I had over 15 years when we decided to start selling hair. We were driving down the street one day and noticed a billboard with a huge hair extension advertisement. I made a comment about how nice it was and my daughter said the ladies that owned the company are pretty young and own several locations. I couldn't believe that selling hair could be that profitable. I thought about it for maybe two minutes and said, I have an idea! Let's sell hair!

My daughter was just as excited as I was and that day marked the changing of our lives.

During our tax season, we invested into a vision that we now call BOSS XTEND. We sought plenty of vendors testing out hair until we found the perfect products to represent our brand. We tested them out by using the hair ourselves and giving it to our friends and family to test. After making our final decision on the perfect product, we immediately started to let everyone we know that we are selling hair!

For the first few months we started selling to our co-workers and friends then branched out to advertising online with social media. As we made more and more sales, we decided to take all our profits and reinvest in more products. We didn't realize that we were sitting on a goldmine. We stocked the hair in our living room and closets until we ran out of space. We then rented a suite inside a salon until we outgrew that space.

I was faced with a decision when I realized that my job with Delta was conflicting with my time to sell hair. I decided to go with my faith and venture full time into my own business.

We rented a second location which became our main location – an 1800 square ft space in Stockbridge, Georgia. We also hired three employees. My sister, a teacher, left her job and came on board expanding our operation into an even bigger organization.

We decided we wanted to create an opportunity for others to start their own businesses without going through as many ups and downs as we had. We started a dropship company called Dropship Lengths for others like us who wanted to change their lives, but didn't know how to do it.

The dropship company took off at a fast rate and we then brought my youngest daughter onto the team. We outgrew our main location and needed to seek some type of warehouse space to hold the inventory and supplies for our dropship customers. The warehouse provided more office space and 4200 square feet of open space. This is our current home today.

We quickly expanded from an idea to a vision and now an active empire of our own creating job opportunities for others like yourself to have their own hair businesses.

If you have ever doubted yourself, take if from us, If we can do it so can you!

Dalandra Young

SPECIAL OFFERS

DROPSHIP LENGTHS

If you're interested in using our Dropship services for your hair company, please visit www.dropshiplengths.com

Email: Dropshiplengths@gmail.com

Phone: 770-626-3937

Powered by Boss Xtend Hair